WHAT ON EARTH IS A
GALAGO
?

EDWARD R. RICCIUTI

 A BLACKBIRCH PRESS BOOK
WOODBRIDGE, CONNECTICUT

Published by Blackbirch Press, Inc.
One Bradley Road, Suite 104
Woodbridge, CT 06525

©1995 Blackbirch Press, Inc.
First Edition

Printed in the United States

10 9 8 7 6 5 4 3 2 1

Photo Credits

Cover, title page: ©Gary Retherford/Photo Researchers, Inc.
Pages 4—5: ©M. Philip Kahl/Photo Researchers, Inc.; page 6: Animals Animals; page 7 (top): ©Blackbirch Press, Inc.; page 7 (bottom): ©Ted Schiffman/Peter Arnold, Inc.; page 9: Stouffer Enterprises, Inc./Animals Animals; page 11: ©M. Reardon/Photo Researchers, Inc.; page 12: ©Stephen Dalton/Animals Animals; pages 14—15: Photo Researchers, Inc.; page 14 (inset): ©S. R. Maglione/Photo Researchers, Inc.; page 16: Photo Researchers, Inc.; page 17 (top): ©Kenneth W. Fink/Photo Researchers, Inc.; page 17 (bottom): ©Nigel Dennis/Photo Researchers, Inc.; page 18: ©George Holton/Photo Researchers, Inc.; pages 20—21: ©Patty Murray/Animals Animals; page 22: ©Mella Panzella/Animals Animals; pages 24—25: ©George Holton/Photo Researchers, Inc.; page 26: ©Tom McHugh/Photo Researchers, Inc.; page 28: ©Michael Dick/Animals Animals; page 29: Stouffer Enterprises, Inc./Animals Animals.

Library of Congress Cataloging-in-Publication Data
Ricciuti, Edward R.
What on earth is a galago? / by Edward R. Ricciuti — 1st ed.
    p.   cm. — (What on earth series)
    Includes bibliographical references (p.   ) and index.
    ISBN 1-56711-101-7
    1. Galagos—Juvenile literature.   [1. Galagos.   2. Primates]
I. Title.   II. Series.
QL737.P93R53   1995
599.8'1—dc20
                                                    94-40356
                                                        CIP
                                                         AC

What does it look like?

Where does it live?

What does it eat?

How does it reproduce?

How does it survive?

TURN THESE PAGES AND FIND OUT!

A galago is a small animal with big, shiny eyes, long hind legs, and a long, furry tail. Galagos are acrobats that can catch small flying insects in mid-air. Galagos also go by another name: bush babies.

A GALAGO, OR BUSH
BABY, IS A SMALL
ANIMAL WITH A VERY
LONG TAIL.

Galagos are members of a group of animals called mammals. Mammals have hair, bear live young, and suckle them on mother's milk. Other mammals include cows, elephants, tigers, whales, and humans. There are six different kinds, or species, of galagos. These species belong to a grouping that scientists call a "family." The galago family is part of a larger group, or class, called primates. Other primates include apes, monkeys, lorises, lemurs, and humans. A galago's hands and feet resemble human hands and feet. Each has five fingers and five toes. Galagos can use their hands and feet to grasp objects, just like many other primates.

OPPOSITE: A GREATER GALAGO
USES ITS HANDS AND FEET TO
CLING TO A TREE BRANCH.
GALAGOS, LIKE CHIMPANZEES
(TOP RIGHT) AND LEMURS
(BOTTOM RIGHT) ARE MAMMALS.

People around the world often use different names for the same animal—calling a galago a "bush baby" is just one example. Sometimes these different names cause confusion. That is why scientists assign special scientific names to each species of animals. "Galagidae" is the name some scientists use for the galago family. The term *galago* comes from an African tribal word that means "monkey." Other scientists, however, believe that galagos and lorises are one family, the "Lorisidae." The name *loris* is believed to come from a Dutch word meaning "slow." Unlike the quick galagos, lorises use slow, deliberate movements to get around.

GALAGOS GET THEIR NAME FROM AN AFRICAN TRIBAL WORD THAT MEANS "MONKEY."

Galagos are little animals. The largest species is only about 1 foot (.3 meter) long and weighs 3 pounds (1.4 kilograms). Other galagos are even smaller. One species is less than 6 inches (15.2 centimeters) long and weighs only a couple of ounces (about 50 grams).

Galagos have large, moveable ears, big, round eyes, and a good sense of smell. Their rear legs are twice the length of their forelegs. Their fingers and toes are tipped with strong, sharp nails, and the undersides of their feet and hands are bare.

The arrangement of slender, sharp teeth in the front of a galago's jaws is rather unusual. Four teeth on top and two on the bottom point forward, instead of up and down. Galagos use these teeth to comb dirt and other materials from their fur. Galagos also clean their fur with the nail on their second toe, which is extra long.

A GALAGO'S LARGE, MOVEABLE EARS HELP IT TO HEAR DIFFERENT NOISES IN ITS SURROUNDINGS.

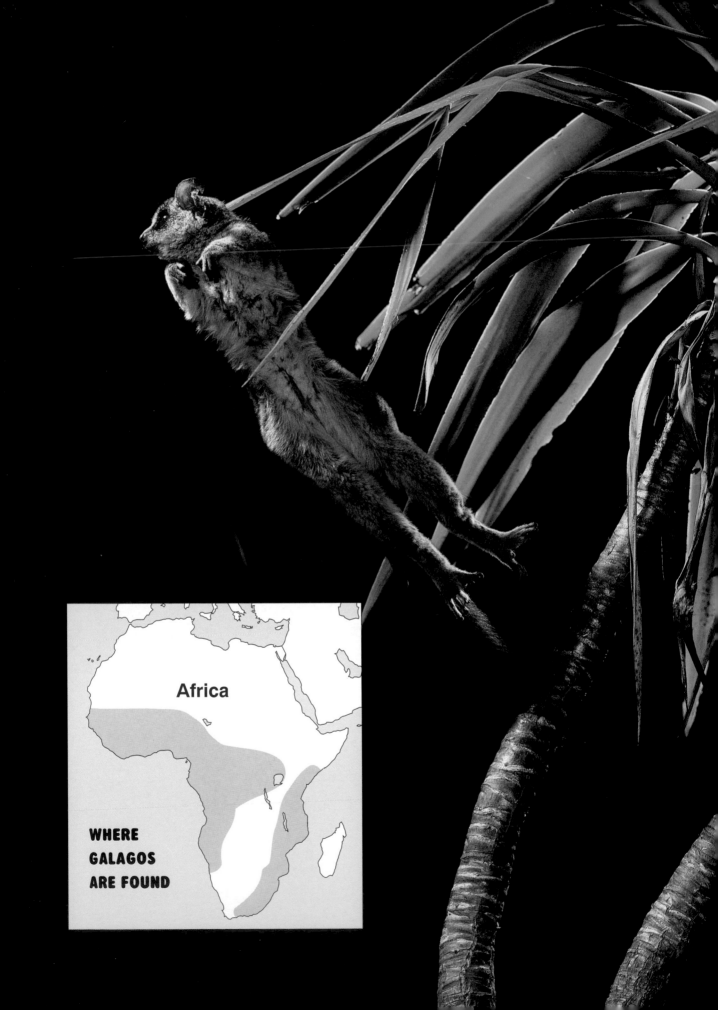

Africa

WHERE
GALAGOS
ARE FOUND

Galagos live in the warm climate of Africa, south of the Sahara Desert. Most species inhabit rainforests, where many trees grow more than 100 feet (30.5 meters) tall. Two species can also be found in scattered woodlands on open, flat plains called the "bush." That, and the fact that some galagos make a sound like a crying baby, is the reason these small primates are commonly called "bush babies."

Galagos usually live high in the trees. Their grasping hands and feet and sharp nails enable them to grab and cling to branches. Galagos are fast and are super jumpers. They often leap up 8 feet (2.4 meters) from branch to branch. The secret of this great leaping ability is a galago's long, powerful hind legs. When a galago is about to jump, it sits in a tight crouch and tenses its muscles. Then its hind legs snap out until fully extended, shooting the animal high into air.

A GALAGO USES ITS
STRONG HIND LEGS
TO LEAP FROM TREE
TO TREE.

Galagos like to feed on tree sap, which they scrape out with their comb-like front teeth. Insects are one of the galago's most important foods. Galagos are so quick that they can catch insects in mid-flight. A galago will sit patiently on a branch waiting for flying insects to approach. When an insect buzzes by, the galago stands, quick as a flash, and grabs it with both hands. This all happens in the blink of an eye.

DURING THE DAY, SOME GALAGOS SLEEP
IN TREE HOLLOWS.

Galagos sleep during the day in tree hollows and on branches. They begin their hunt for food once it is dark. Finding food in a dark forest is not easy, but the galago's good sense of smell helps. In addition, their large, round eyes help them gather whatever light is available from the moon and stars. A galago's eye can even use the same light twice. In the rear of the eye is a layer of cells that reflects light, like a mirror. Light that enters the eye bounces off this cell layer, which allows the eye to use the light a second time.

Galago ears are also very helpful for hunting in the dark. These moveable, cup-like ears can be focused in different directions to collect sounds.

A vast number of other animals live in the African forests inhabited by galagos. The forests are home to many different kinds of snakes, birds, and an enormous number of insects. Other animal neighbors include elephants, leopards, monkeys, wild pigs, as well as mongooses and their relatives, civets and genets.

LEOPARDS
(OPPOSITE) AND
COLORFUL BIRDS
SHARE THE GALAGO'S
HOME IN THE
AFRICAN FOREST.

Civets and genets are animals that look like a cross between a cat and a weasel. They are good climbers, and they hunt at night. Civets and genets will often hunt galagos. Owls—night creatures—also kill and eat galagos. There are probably other animals that hunt galagos as well, but because galagos live so high in trees deep within wild forests, it has been difficult for scientists to study and discover the galago's other natural enemies.

AN AFRICAN GENET,
LIKE A GALAGO, IS AN
EXCELLENT CLIMBER.

Hunting and moving about at night is good protection for galagos. If they were out during the day, eagles and hawks could easily prey on them. However, eagles and hawks do not hunt at night. The same senses that help galagos find food—smell, hearing, and sight—also alert them to the presence of possible enemies. When in danger, a galago's only real defense is to flee, leaping away as fast as possible, and hiding high in the branches. As it does, it utters loud, high-pitched cries, which tell other galagos that danger is near.

TO ESCAPE
THEIR ENEMIES,
GALAGOS WILL
HIDE IN THICK
TREE BRANCHES.

Galagos generally live in small groups, usually one or two females and their young. Sometimes these females live with an adult male. Most males, however, live on their own. Each group has its own territory, or home range. Galagos mark the location of their territories with their urine. Most species put urine on their hands and feet, so that the scent is left behind as galagos travel from branch to branch. A few species urinate on branches. Many scientists believe that the urine scent may also help males find females when it is time to mate.

Usually, a galago male will travel through the territories of several females and will try to mate with those that are ready to mate. Males sometimes fight over females. The strongest males get the most mates.

TWO GALAGOS SHARE
A HOLLOWED-OUT LOG.
GALAGOS OFTEN LIVE
TOGETHER IN SMALL
GROUPS.

Galagos mate just like all other mammals. While mating, the male deposits his sex cells, or sperm, inside the female. When a sperm joins with a female sex cell, or egg, a new individual begins to form. The joining of the sperm and egg is called fertilization. The fertilized egg develops into an embryo. A galago embryo grows for about three months inside the mother's body, developing into a young galago.

A MALE AND FEMALE GALAGO
COME TOGETHER TO MATE.

AFTER A FEW MONTHS, YOUNG GALAGOS WILL REACH THEIR ADULT SIZE.

A female galago usually gives birth to one offspring at a time, in a nest of leaves and sticks. Sometimes, twins are born. Newborn galagos are tiny, less than an ounce (28 grams) in weight. At first, they cannot travel on their own. However, they are soon able to follow their mother around as she jumps among the branches. The young live on their mother's milk for about two months. After that time, they eat the same foods as adults. In less than a year, they are fully adult and ready to mate.

AN EAST AFRICAN GARNETTS GALAGO WATCHES FOR SIGNS OF DANGER.

Since galagos live deep in the forest, and are active only at night, they have little direct contact with humans. In the past, however, they were occasionally captured and sold as pets. Galagos are cute animals, and can be tamed, but they do not make good pets. Pet owners cannot provide the wild surroundings and conditions that galagos need to survive. In addition, galagos sleep all day and are active at night. This schedule does not suit most pet owners.

Today, almost every country in the world has agreed not to import galagos for sale as pets. The capture of galagos for commercial purposes did not greatly reduce their numbers, but, even so, the population is declining. Dwarf galagos are now on the list of endangered species and are in great danger of disappearing. The main reason for this serious drop in population is that people are destroying the forest in which galagos live. Trees are being cut for lumber and to make room for farming and other kinds of development. Large areas of forest must be protected if galagos and the animals that share their home are to survive in the future.

A DWARF GALAGO CLIMBS THROUGH THE FOREST. MANY GALAGOS HAVE HAD THEIR HABITATS DESTROYED BECAUSE OF LAND DEVELOPMENT.

Glossary

egg Female sex cell.

embryo The developing organism that forms from the fertilized egg.

fertilization The joining of sperm and egg that creates the embryo.

loris A close relative of galagos.

mammals The group of animals, including people, that produce their own body heat, have hair, and feed their young on mother's milk.

primates The class of mammals to which galagos belong.

species A group of living things that are closely related to one another. Members of a species can reproduce with one another.

sperm Male sex cell.

Further Reading

Bogard, Vicki. *Monkeys, Apes and Other Primates*. Ossining, NY: Young Discovery Library, 1989.

Brooks, F. *Protecting Endangered Species*. Tulsa, OK: EDC Publishing, 1991.

Chinery, Michael. *Rainforest Animals*. New York: Random, 1992.

Cunningham, Antonia. *Rainforest Wildlife*. Tulsa, OK: EDC Publishing, 1993.

Ganeri, Anita. *Small Mammals*. Chicago: Watts, 1993.

Lambert, David. *The Golden Concise Encyclopedia of Mammals*. New York: Western, 1992.

Parsons, Alexandra. *Amazing Mammals*. New York: Random House, 1990.

Purcell, John W. *African Animals*. Chicago: Childrens, 1982.

The Sierra Club Book of Small Mammals. San Francisco: Sierra, 1993.

Tesar, Jenny. *Mammals*. Woodbridge, CT: Blackbirch Press, Inc., 1993.

Index

Africa, 13, 16
Ape, 7

Bush baby, 4, 13
  See also Galago.

Civet, 16, 19

Dwarf galago, 29

Galago
  defense, 20
  ears, 10, 15
  enemies, 19
  eyes, 4, 10, 15
  feet, 7, 10, 13
  food, 4, 14, 15
  hands, 7, 10, 13
  hearing (sense of), 20
  legs, 4, 10, 13
  length, 10
  mating, 23, 24, 27
  newborn, 27
  scientific name, 8
  sight (sense of), 20
  smell (sense of), 10, 15, 20
  tail, 4
  teeth, 10, 14
  territory, 23
  urine, 23
  weight, 10
Genet, 16, 19

Lemur, 7
Leopard, 16
Loris, 7, 8

Mongoose, 16
Monkey, 7, 16